UNDERSTANDING
CHRISTIANITY

ORIGINS BELIEFS PRACTICES HOLY TEXTS SACRED PLACES

UNDERSTANDING
CHRISTIANITY

RIGINS BELIEFS PRACTICES HOLY TEXTS SACRED PLACES

ROSEMARY DRAGE HALE

WATKINS PUBLISHING
LONDON

Understanding Christianity
Rosemary Drage Hale

This edition first published in the United Kingdom and Ireland in 2010 by
Watkins Publishing, an imprint of Duncan Baird Publishers
Sixth Floor, Castle House, 75–76 Wells Street, London, W1T 3QH

Conceived, created and designed by Duncan Baird Publishers

British Library Cataloguing-in-Publication Data:
A CIP record for this book is available from the British Library

Library of Congress Cataloging-in-Publication Data

Hale, Rosemary Drage.
  Understanding Christianity : origins, beliefs, practices, holy texts, sacred places / Rosemary Drage Hale.
    p. cm.
  Includes bibliographical references (p.   ) and index.
  ISBN 978-1-907486-15-9 (alk. paper)
  1. Christianity. I. Title.
  BR121.3 .H35
  230--dc22
                        2010002378

ISBN: 978-1-907486-15-9

10 9 8 7 6 5 4 3 2 1

Typeset in Garamond Three
Colour reproduction by Scanhouse, Malaysia
Printed and bound in Thailand by Imago

NOTES
The abbreviations BCE and CE are used throughout this book:
BCE Before the Common Era (the equivalent of BC)
CE Common Era (the equivalent of AD)

Page 2: Dawn service in the church of St. Madeleine, Vézelay, Burgundy, France.

Distributed in the USA and Canada by
Sterling Publishing Co., Inc.
387 Park Avenue South
New York, NY 10016-8810

For information about custom editions, special sales, premium and corporate purchases, please
contact Sterling Special Sales Department at 800-805-5489 or specialsales@sterlingpub.com.

CONTENTS

INTRODUCTION

Shortly after the crucifixion (ca. 30CE) of Jesus of Nazareth, a Jewish preacher and healer, a new religious movement emerged that was to change that world forever. An inner circle of Jesus' disciples and many of his followers believed him to be the Christ, or Messiah, a divine redeemer of humankind, who had been resurrected after his death. From this "Jesus movement" emerged the Christian faith, now the largest of the world's religions, with nearly two billion adherents spread over almost every country.

Essentially, Christianity is a monotheistic tradition centered on faith in one God and in Jesus Christ as the savior and redeemer of humankind. Christianity holds that God became incarnate—fully human—in Jesus of Nazareth. Christians believe that Jesus died on a cross and was resurrected. The belief in the Trinity, the sacred mystery of Father, Son, and Holy Spirit as one, triune ("three-in-one") God, is central to the Christian tradition.

There are hundreds of Christian groups, or "denominations," the primary ones being Roman Catholicism (the largest branch of the faith), Eastern Orthodoxy, and Protestantism. Broadly speaking, Catholics subscribe to the authority of an infallible pope as the head of the church. Their worship is elaborately liturgical and focuses on seven "sacraments" (acts considered to confer divine grace)—baptism, Eucharist (the Lord's Supper, or Holy Communion), confirmation, penance, matrimony, priestly ordination, and extreme unction (anointing the dying). The veneration of saints plays a major part in Catholic devotional practice.

Eastern Orthodoxy, in ways similar to Roman Catholicism, maintains a strong historical continuity with the early church, but resists the notion of authority vested in a single leader. Instead, the Orthodox churches are governed by bishops, patriarchs (senior bishops), and councils. In contrast to Roman Catholicism, Orthodox priests may marry provided they do so before ordination. Orthodox worship also centers on the sacraments and is notable for the use of icons as aids to spirituality.

The Protestant movement dates from the sixteenth century, when Martin Luther and other Christian reformers rejected a great many aspects of the Roman church. Protestantism has developed into a hugely diverse branch of Christianity, embracing a remarkable number of offshoots and a great range of views on church governance, styles of worship, requirements for ministry, and attitudes toward the Eucharist, saints, baptism, and salvation. However, all Protestants reject the authority of the pope and would agree on the primary authority of the Bible.

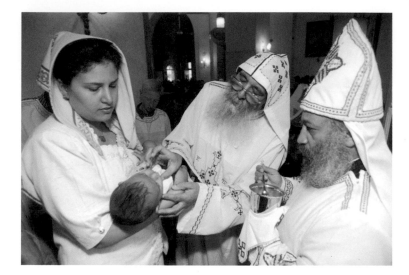

An infant, held by its mother, is tended by clergymen during a Coptic (Egyptian Christian) mass in Bilyana, Egypt. The Coptic Church is based on the teachings of St. Mark, who brought Christianity to Egypt in the first century CE.

They recognize only two sacraments (baptism and the Lord's Supper), although for some Protestant churches even these are more symbolic than sacramental. Generally the laity takes a much more active role than is permitted in Catholicism.

As recently as a generation ago, those who identified themselves as "Catholic," "Methodist," "Baptist," and so on, could generally be assumed to share a broad world-view with others of the same denomination. This is no longer the case. Issues such as homosexuality, inclusive language, women's ordination, and abortion are widely debated. Today, in many churches, "fundamentalists" and "liberals" stand in opposition to each other.

However, there are also strong forces that seek to stress Christian unity, or "ecumenism." Since 1948, the World Council of Churches has sought to draw together churches that accept Jesus Christ as God and savior. This body advises such organizations as the United Nations and carries out an extensive world aid program.

Despite the sometimes radical differences that have marked interdenominational relations, there are a number of issues upon which all Christians would tentatively agree, in addition to the tradition's basic theology and scriptures. All would hold that community and fellowship are vital to Christian worship. There would be accord on the essential Christian virtues—"faith, hope, and love" (1 Corinthians 13.13)—and on the belief that a life lived as far as possible in imitation of Jesus is "the Christian way." In the main, Christianity is life-affirming. The incarnation of God as Christ is symbolized as light in the darkness of the world, and the Resurrection is regarded as a joyful affirmation of hope, demonstrating the love of God for his creation.

CHAPTER ONE

ORIGINS AND HISTORICAL DEVELOPMENT

The foundational story of the birth, life, death, and resurrection of Jesus is at the heart of all Christian denominations. Chiefly preserved in the four New Testament gospels of Matthew, Mark, Luke, and John and intended as proclamations about Jesus as son of God and redeemer of humankind, the gospels do not easily lend themselves to historical scholarship. Nevertheless, it is generally agreed that the founder of Christianity, Jesus Christ, was born during the reign of Herod the Great to a woman named Mary and her spouse, Joseph, who was raised in Nazareth in northern Palestine. Both were pious Jews. Complex historical developments have resulted in a wide variety of practices and beliefs among today's Christian denominations that reflect intense and lively reforms throughout the centuries.

LEFT:
Detail from Christ the Redeemer, *a 13th-century icon from the Chilandar monastery, Mount Athos, Greece.*

The biblical accounts of Jesus' nativity and his adult baptism create an aura of divine mystery. The baptism marked the beginning of his public ministry when he took on twelve chief disciples, the apostles. After his death they were regarded as his successors and held responsible for spreading the belief in him as messiah and redeemer. The gospels tell of Jesus as a wonder-working prophet—the stories of his many miracles were regarded by his followers as evidence of his messiahship.

There is broad consensus that in Jerusalem, at the time of the Jewish festival of Passover, Jesus was betrayed by one of his followers and arrested. After cross-examination by the Jewish authorities, he was sent before the Roman governor, Pontius Pilate, and found guilty of claiming to be king of the Jews, a claim that was blasphemous under Jewish law and treason to the Romans. Jesus was sentenced to death by crucifixion.

But the Jesus movement did not die out with its leader's death. Shortly after his crucifixion, a small group of Jews began to proclaim that Jesus had been resurrected, and that in his resurrection the messianic hopes of Israel had been fulfilled. They could hardly have foreseen the astounding success of their preaching.

Christianity was to achieve its greatest success in the conversion of non-Jews, but it emerged unequivocally from the tradition of Judaism. While most believers following the Crucifixion were Palestinian Jews, within two decades of his death the mission to the non-Jews (gentiles) was well underway. The story of this mission begins with a Greek-speaking Diaspora Jew and Roman citizen, Saul of Tarsus (whose Greek name was Paul). Saul/Paul began as a persecutor, assisting at the stoning of Stephen—revered as the first Christian martyr—in Jerusalem. Shortly afterward, he experienced a vision of Jesus and converted (Acts 9.1–19, 22.5–16). He then began a zealous, lifelong, and successful mission to convert the gentiles of Greece and Asia Minor. Paul was one of the first to articulate a Christian theology distinct from Jewish practice and law.

Early Christianity faced several obstacles. Christians refused to sacrifice to the Greco-Roman deities or to acknowledge the Roman emperor as a god, as required by law. Hence, simply being a Christian was treason and many Christians were martyred, but their example served to advertise the new religion and to unify its followers. Persecution effectively ended after the emperor Constantine's Edict of Milan (313CE) decreed tolerance for all religions. In 392CE, Theodosius I declared Christianity the sole religion of the empire.

The rise of Christianity coincides with the "Patristic" era named after the Fathers of the Church (*Patres Ecclesiae*), the great theologians whose works helped shape Christian thought and doctrine. Perhaps the most influential of these was St. Augustine (354–430CE), bishop of Hippo in north Africa. Bishops had been instituted early in this period to act as spiritual heads of Christian communities, with those of Rome, Antioch, Jerusalem, Alexandria, and Constantinople regarded as the "patriarchs" of the church.

The terms "heretic" and "heresy" refer to Christians who disagreed with orthodox doctrine and belief. In order to flourish, the early church needed to formulate a uniform system of beliefs and a fixed canon of scripture. Ecclesiastical orthodoxy was determined by bishops and theologians meeting to discuss such issues as the nature of the Trinity, priestly celibacy, the role of women, scriptural authority, and the form of the liturgy.

For the first five centuries, the church remained as one. Two issues created a schism between the East (Orthodox) and West (Roman) churches—the question of papal authority and devotion to icons. In 1054, a Byzantine community refused to pay homage to Pope Leo IX and this led to the excommunication of the Eastern church. The two churches have never been reunited.

Western Christianity continued to expand during a succession of crusades from 1095—military expeditions aimed at the expulsion of Muslims from the Holy Land. The interaction with Islamic civilization also brought Western culture into contact, via Arab scholarship, with the lost philosophical traditions of ancient Greece, especially Aristotle. This rediscovery brought renewed vigor to Christian philosophy, reflected in the work of theologians whose collective approach is referred to as "scholasticism." The greatest scholastic thinker was probably St. Thomas Aquinas (1225–74; see p.27).

The medieval flowering of Christian scholarship coincided with the rise of universities in Europe, and with the reform of the long tradition of Benedictine monasticism. St. Benedict of Nursia (480–550CE), founder of the Benedictine order, wrote a set of spiritual guidelines for monks and nuns. The Rule of St. Benedict still serves as the basis for Western monasticism and includes regulations for the hours of sleep, manual work, reading, and mealtimes. Thirteenth-century monastic reforms resulted in the emergence of several new orders as well as the formation of the mendicant ("begging") orders of the Dominicans and Franciscans, who originally sought to lead poor and humble lives in imitation of Jesus and his disciples.

A *manuscript illumination depicting the four Evangelists (Matthew, Mark, Luke, and John), from a set of 9th-century Viennese coronation gospel books.*

Reformers such as John Wyclif (or Wycliffe, 1330–84) in England and John (Jan) Hus (1373–1415) in Bohemia prepared the way for the major reforms of Martin Luther (1483–1546), an Augustinian friar of Wittenberg, Germany, who publicly posted ninety-five "theses," criticizing Rome for selling indulgences (see pp.20–21). In spite of church opposition, the German reform movement quickly gathered pace and within just a few years the split in Western Christianity had become irrevocable. In 1529, the signatories to one formal protest against the suppression of reformers were dubbed "Protestants," and this name stuck.

Protestantism, which essentially advocated the authority of scripture over that of an ecclesiastical hierarchy, developed along several distinct lines. Radical reformers such as Ulrich Zwingli (1484–1531) and John Calvin (1509–64) opposed the veneration of images, certain aspects of the Roman liturgy, and clerical celibacy. Unlike those who followed Luther's notion of salvation through faith and not through deeds, Calvin believed in predestination: some of the faithful were destined to be saved, others were not. The origin of one of the largest denominations, Anglicanism (the Church of England and its affiliates, such as Episcopalianism), was linked with the pope's refusal of a divorce to King Henry VIII (ruled 1509–47).

The Protestant Reformation prompted a renewal of Roman Catholicism that is known as the "Counter-Reformation." Fostered by the Council of Trent (1545–63), the Catholic reform movement saw not only the end of many of the practices (such as the sale of indulgences; see pp.20–21) that had fired the reformers, but also the founding of new orders such as the intellectually rigorous Society of Jesus (the Jesuits), who, under the guidance of their founder, Ignatius of Loyola (1491–1556), sought to lay new emphasis on pastoral care and missionary work. The Counter-Reformation also led to a reaffirmation of the supremacy of priests, the sacraments, and the authority of the papacy in those areas where it remained dominant. The New World, America, provided refuge for many experiencing religious persecution at home. The era of the Reformation and Counter-Reformation coincided with the beginnings of European colonialism. As Europeans expanded their horizons globally, missionaries zealous to "make disciples of all nations" (Matthew 28.19), had a profound impact on the worldwide spread of Christianity.

Today, the term Protestant covers an extraordinary proliferation of denominations. The major churches of Protestantism include Lutherans, Baptists, Methodists,

Presbyterians, Anglicans (or Episcopalians), Friends United Meeting (Quakers), Mennonites, Mormons, and Christian Scientists. Among other groups, Seventh-Day Adventists celebrate the Sabbath on Saturday and adhere to some of the dietary laws of the Old Testament. Denominations such as Jehovah's Witnesses are called "millennialist," because they believe that Christ will return for the final apocalyptic battle of Armageddon, after which he will reign for a thousand years. Evangelicalism is common to several Protestant churches. Evangelicals typically regard themselves as "born again" in Christ. One of the fastest growing movements is Pentecostalism. The term refers to the descent of the Holy Spirit among the apostles at the time of the Pentecost and has a strong focus on evangelism, is essentially charismatic and relates to ecstatic experiences.

Urbanization and secularization, particularly in the West, contributed to a change in the traditional functions performed by the church in earlier historical periods. Nonetheless, the vitality of the Christian faith is evidenced in a continual process of reform and internal pluralism. Today, more than 400 denominations all identify themselves as Christian. Many regard this worldwide religious diversity as one of the greatest challenges facing Christianity in the modern world.

Martin Luther's Disputation on Indulgences

" 25. The general power which the pope has over purgatory, is ... no different from the power which any ... bishop or priest has, within his own bishopric or parish; [...]

33. Men must be on careful guard against those who say that the papal indulgences are an inestimable gift of God and that a man is reconciled to God by them; [...]

36. Every Christian who is truly repentant enjoys full remission of penalty and guilt even without letters of indulgence;

37. Every true Christian ... shares in all the blessings of Christ and the Church; and this is granted him by God, even without letters of indulgence; [...]

41. Papal indulgences are to be preached with caution, lest people wrongly think them preferable to other good works of love;

42. [T]he pope does not intend the buying of indulgences as comparable in any way to acts of mercy;

43. [H]e who gives to the poor or lends to the needy does a better deed than buying indulgences;

44. [B]y the deeds of love, love grows and one becomes a better man; whereas by buying indulgences, he does not become a better man ... only free from certain penalties. **"**

Martin Luther's "Disputation on the Power and Efficacy of Indulgences," October 31, 1517, from the Latin *Disputatio Declaratione Virtutis Indulgentiarum.* Martin Luthers Werke. 1 Band. Herman Baehlau: Weimar, 1883, pp.233–38, translated by Rosemary Drage Hale.

Commentary

These statements come from a document essential to the formation of Protestantism—Martin Luther's "Disputation on the Power and Efficacy of Indulgences." Luther was convinced that the people of his parish were being misled into believing that they could purchase salvation through the buying of what were called indulgences. According to the popular tradition, in October 1517, Luther posted the ninety-five propositions for debate on the door of his church in Wittenburg, Germany. They are credited with having a lasting impact on Christianity.

The practice of granting indulgences, whereby venial sins normally punished in purgatory would be forgiven, had a long history in Christianity. During the First Crusade, the pope granted soldiers plenary indulgences for their service to the Church. By the mid-sixteenth century, the Church was selling indulgences throughout Europe and the abuse of the practice was the catalyst for the Reformation. Martin Luther's argument concerning indulgences was the basis of a more profound disagreement with Roman Catholicism at the time. He believed that humanity's relationship to God did not depend on the Church's mediation through sacraments, but rather on the believer's own faith in God and the salvific act of His son.

CHAPTER TWO

ASPECTS OF THE DIVINE

"In the beginning was the Word, and the Word was with God, and the Word was God ... And the Word became flesh and lived among us, and we have seen His glory." Many modern scholars contest the authenticity of the opening lines of the gospel of John. However, few would question their importance for an understanding of the origins of Christianity. The lines echo the opening of the Hebrew Bible, "In the beginning God created the heavens and the earth," but they also reveal a critical difference between Christianity and Judaism. In John's words, the divinity is created in the flesh, in the human nature of Jesus of Nazareth, who is regarded as the Son of God, redeemer of humankind. One of the essential mysteries of the tradition, the godhead in Christianity is considered to be both divine and human.

LEFT:
The Holy Trinity, by a 14th-century Hungarian painter known as the Master of the Trinity. God the Father, enthroned, holds the crucified Son, above whose head hovers the Holy Spirit in the form of a white dove.

Christian theology is profoundly complex and has a great many forms and methods. However, it can be broadly divided into two types: dogmatic theology and moral theology. Dogmatic theology, the science of the theoretical truths of God, seeks to establish fundamental doctrines and articles of faith. Drawing on scripture and tradition, dogmatic theology generally deals with issues relating to the concept of the Trinity. The Trinity is a central doctrine of Christianity and has challenged theologians throughout the history of the religion. The doctrine holds that there is one God but that God comprises three elements—Father, Son, and Holy Spirit—worshipped as a unity.

It is generally agreed that the Bible contains no explicit teaching of the Trinity. The gospels of Matthew, Mark, and Luke emphasize Christ's humanity, while the gospel of John stresses his divinity. Early theologians were keen to stress Jesus' divine nature, but debated how Christianity could remain monotheistic if both Jesus and God were to be regarded as divine. As early as the second century CE, Tertullian (155–222CE) used the term *trinitas* (Latin, "trinity") in theological discourse, teaching that God is "one substance" comprised of "three persons." Origen (185–254CE) insisted that Christian faith is founded on the unity of a transcendent

God (who created humanity), coeternal with the Son (who redeemed humanity) and the Spirit (who sanctified humanity). By the fourth century CE, theologians had consolidated the orthodox position of God as three persons in one nature and placed this doctrine in the opening lines of the statement of faith known as the "Athanasian Creed."

The Cappadocian Fathers—theologians of Asia Minor whose writings remain vital and doctrinally sound for Eastern Orthodoxy—differed from the West on the issue of the generation of the Son and the "procession" of the Holy Spirit. One doctrinal issue at the center of the East-West schism was the East's insistence that the Spirit "proceeded" (originated, or arose) from the Father *through* the Son, while the West insisted on procession from the Father *and* the Son.

Moral theology, while grounded in Christian dogma, is the science of practical moral truths and aims to explain the divine laws and the relationship of humankind to God. Christian theological inquiry has had a lively history that goes back to the beginnings of the church. Within an expansive general brief—"the nature of God"—theologians systematically treat a wide range of topics relevant to doctrinal concerns.

There is theological discourse in the New Testament,

The Ecstasy of St. Theresa, *by Gian Lorenzo Bernini (1598–1680; altarpiece detail). The sculpture depicts the saint's soul being pierced with God's love (here represented as Cupid).*

but the distinct discipline of theology emerged only with the "Church Fathers," such as St. Augustine, in the early years of Christianity.

Centuries later, with the development of European universities in the Middle Ages, theology was placed at the pinnacle of studies as "Queen of the Sciences." This was the period of "scholastic" theology, a systematized manner of deriving theological conclusions on the basis of "syllogism" (deductive reasoning). Foremost among the scholastic theologians is Thomas Aquinas (1225–74), author of *Summa Theologica* ("The Sum of Theology"), a work of profound influence that attempts to synthesize reason and faith in the light of western Europe's rediscovery, via Muslim scholarship, of ancient Greek philosophy.

After the Protestant Reformations and the Enlightenment, theological inquiry diversified and the plurality of thought was compounded by the emergence of various denominational perspectives. Critical reason and scientific advancements further challenged theological thought. Friedrich Schleiermacher (1768–1834), hailed as the founder of Protestant theology, argued that theology could not be circumscribed by reason and morality, but rather by the human feeling of dependence upon an infinite being. Ludwig Feuerbach, author of *Essence of Christianity* (1841), claimed that God is a mental projection whose purpose is to respond to human hopes and satisfy human needs. In the twentieth century, Paul Tillich (1886–1965) saw Christian theology in the context of the modern world, maintaining that Christian faith is one of many ways of dealing with the "ultimate concern" of existence and God. The history of Christian theology is an elaborate story of varied interpretations and reconstructions of the mysteries of the faith.

Christian mysticism is essentially theistic, that is, it centers on the transcendent reality of God and typically emphasizes divine love. Overall, it is shaped by Christian notions of God and reflects God's relationship to the soul. The expansive writing of Christian mystics is often divided into two strands: the intellectual discussion of mystical philosophy and the experiential descriptions of practical mysticism. Regardless of type, a common theme in Christian mystical literature is that of the inexpressibility or ineffability of the mystic union with God. Philosophical mysticism analyzes the nature of divine union while practical mysticism tends to use metaphorical language to describe the experience itself.

While personal narratives of Christian mystical experience vary widely, all Christian mystics describe in some way or another a direct awareness of the presence of God, generally defined by scholars and theologians as "mystical union" (Latin, *unio mystica*) with God. Mystical union often involves a lengthy preparation, a life path beginning with an "awakening," followed by a period of purgation, an "illumination," and finally the experience of union. For others, it is a transcendent experience that comes suddenly, without preparation, but utterly transforms their lives. The mystic's spiritual path is inward, turned away from the world.

The roots of Christian mysticism are scriptural. Paul, in particular, taught that through the love of Christ, the Christian may experience the presence of God. Nonetheless, while early Christian mysticism included a prominent contemplative element, it was essentially intellectual and philosophical and drew on Greek and Roman thought.

The medieval church saw a flourishing of mystical experience. Mystics perceived themselves as instruments of God, and while they led contemplative lives, popes and secular rulers solicited their counsel. The many famous mystics of the period include the remarkable Hildegard of Bingen (1098–1179), a German abbess who recounted her prophetic and apocalyptic visions using allegorical symbols. The French mystic St. Bernard of Clairvaux (1090–1153) employed the imagery of the Song of Songs in the Bible to portray the union of the soul and Christ in terms of a metaphorical marriage. In Italy, St. Francis of Assisi (1181–1226), founder of the Franciscan monastic order, practiced a mysticism based on the "imitation of Christ." In her account of her revelations on the mystery of the faith, Julian of Norwich (1342–ca. 1415), one of many medieval English mystics, focused on the infinity and immeasurability of divine love and employed the metaphor of Christ as mother.

There are innumerable reports of devotees attaining a state of mystic ecstasy accompanied by various physical manifestations such as swooning, levitation, weeping fits, and trance. Such states are said to arise from divine activity within the soul and are attended by alienated or heightened senses. In the thirteenth century, when devotion to the suffering Christ was especially culti-vated, St. Francis became the first mystic to receive stigmata, the marks of the five wounds of the crucified Christ. St. Theresa of Avila, a sixteenth-century Spanish mystic, reformer, and organizer of the Carmelite order, maintained that ecstatic experience was one stage on the way to mystical union with God. Her autobiographical writings and treatise on the mystical path, *The Interior Castle*, were composed during the tumultuous times of the Spanish Inquisition and so offer only cautious descriptions of the stages of ecstasy and rapture.

Contemplative mysticism is central to Eastern Orthodoxy and is based on a meditative technique for divine union that involves the constant repetition of "the Jesus Prayer": "Lord Jesus Christ have mercy on me a sinner." The prayer dates from the fifth century CE and is still recited in Orthodox churches. The devotional practice of repeating the Jesus Prayer is called "hesychasm" (from the Greek for "quietness"). Practitioners report that it produces a state of spiritual stillness in which they have an experience of holy wisdom, a partaking of the nature of God. A famous Greek saint and mystic, Gregory of Palamas (1296–1359), was among those to recount this direct communion with the divine. By saying the prayer, the worshipper also hopes to experience a vision of the Divine Light, thought to be identical with the light of the Transfiguration (Matthew 17.1–9 and parallel passages in Mark and Luke).

Following the Reformation, Protestant views of mysticism were generally negative, but some Protestants, such as the Lutheran Jakob Boehme (1575–1624), did recount experiences of mystical divine union. One of the most influential of Protestant mystics, Boehme claimed to have experienced knowledge of the nature of the Trinity. In more recent times, Christian mystics have drawn on mystical traditions outside Christianity. Thomas Merton (1915–68), for example, was inspired by Buddhism. The appeal of mysticism remains vibrant today as Christians continue to find inspiration in their efforts to communicate the profound and intense mystery of the soul's union with God.

The Chalcedonian Definition of Jesus' Identity

66 We all with one voice confess our Lord Jesus Christ
to be one and the same Son perfect in divinity and
humanity, truly God and truly human, consisting of
a rational soul and a body, being of one substance with
the Father in relation to his divinity, and being of one
substance with us in relation to his humanity, and is
like us in all things apart from sin. He was begotten
of the Father before time in relation to his divinity, and
in these recent days was born from the Virgin Mary, for
us and for our salvation. In relation to the humanity, he
is one and the same Christ, the Son, the Lord, the Only
Begotten who is to be acknowledged in two natures,
without confusion, without change, without division,
and without separation. This distinction of natures
is in no way abolished on account of this union, but
rather the characteristic property of each nature is
preserved, and concurring into one Person and one
subsistence, not as if Christ were parted or divided into
two persons, but remains one and the same Son and
only-begotten God, Word, Lord Jesus Christ. 99

From *The Oecumenical Documents of the Faith* by T.H. Bradley and F.W. Green. London: Metheun, 1950. pp.85ff.

Commentary

The first centuries of Christianity saw many controversies over the substance and identity of Jesus. In 325CE the bishops met as an ecumenical council in Nicaea to attempt to resolve the issue. The primary concern of the Council of Nicaea was to comprehend the New Testament references to the relationship of Christ as the *Logos,* or the Word, and his relationship to God, the Father. The Council ended with a creedal statement that has lasted centuries: "We believe in one God, the Father Almighty, Maker of all things visible and invisible. And, in one Lord, Jesus Christ, the Son of God, begotten of the Father, Light of Light, very God of very God, begotten not made, being of one substance with the Father ... and the Holy Ghost."

Called the Nicene Creed, this statement brought about the Arian controversy, a vigorous debate over the relation of the humanity and divinity of Christ. In 451, the Eastern Emperor Marcian gathered another council of bishops at Chalcedon to resolve the controversy. more than 500 bishops agreed on the Chalcedonian Definition as to the identity of Jesus, that he was one person consisting of two natures. The Council's Definition is regarded as a watershed in the history of Christianity and a turning point in Christological theology.

Clara doctri
na grata fa
cundia preci
pue circa sen
sū literalem
necessaria

CHAPTER THREE

SACRED TEXTS

There are a number of texts, including prayers, hymns, and liturgies, that hold a special place in the hearts of Christians, but for a theistic tradition, such as Christianity, scripture will be a central and sacred text. The Bible is regarded by Christians as having been inspired by God and is thus Christianity's holiest text. Recitations from both the Old and New Testaments figure prominently in the worship of all Christian services throughout the liturgical year. The Bible is considered to be a literary work, an historical document, and a major source of theological doctrine. In some families, it is more than a treasured book—it is also a significant heirloom, as it is sometimes the place in which the family tree is outlined and where important events, such as births and deaths, are recorded.

LEFT:
St. Jerome, by Pedro Berruguete (1450–1504). St. Jerome was a scholar and churchman who spent the majority of his life translating the Bible from Greek into Latin. His translation, known as the Vulgate, was the definitive edition of the Bible that was used in the West until the Reformation.

Comprised of sixty-six books, the Bible consists of two parts: the "Old Testament," essentially the Hebrew Bible, which for Christianity represents God's first covenant with humankind; and the "New Testament," the covenant of Jesus Christ, in whom God's promises to Israel were fulfilled. The Old Testament is a remarkably complex work and includes the Pentateuch or the five books of law, the historical books, wisdom literature, and the books of the prophets. For Christians, the Old Testament narrates God's self-revelation in the world prior to the coming of Jesus Christ.

The New Testament, composed in the century following Christ's death, records his birth, ministry, passion ("suffering"), and resurrection. It also contains "Acts of the Apostles," including an account of Paul's mission to the gentiles, and letters by Paul and other figures in the early church. The last book, Revelation, is an apocalyptic vision of the end of time. At the core of the compilation are the four "gospels" (an old English word translating Greek *euangelion*, "good news") attributed to authors called Matthew, Mark, Luke, and John (the "evangelists"). Since the late eighteenth century, scholars have referred to the first three gospels as "synoptic" ("viewed together"), because when looked at in tandem they are seen to contain many significant parallels. The gospel of

John, or the "Fourth Gospel" (ca. 95CE), is markedly different in style and tone. Collectively, the four books are called simply "the Gospel."

Continuity between the Old and New Testaments is both cultural and theological. How both together came to constitute the authorized scripture of Christianity is a complex story. Christians and Jews share most of the texts of the Hebrew Bible, but the early church reordered them so as to conclude the Old Testament with the books of the prophets. The Old Testament thus ends with the book of Malachi, whose reference to the prophet Elijah as precursor of the messiah was understood by the gospel writers to apply to John the Baptist (Matthew 11.7–15 and Luke 1.16–17).

The canon of the New Testament consists of writings that the early church considered to have been inspired by God, and saw as best communicating the religious experience of Christians. It was not the work of a single individual or a church council, but evolved piecemeal over several centuries. As early as 160CE, the theologian Tertullian used the phrase "New Testament" to refer to a collection of first-century writings recalling Christ. But it was not until the early fifth century that the twenty-seven books of today's New Testament gained universal acceptance and that the Christian canon attained a form

A copy of the illuminated first page of the gospel of St. Luke from the Gutenberg Bible. The manuscript includes hand-painted initials and ornaments. Mainz, 1455.

recognizable to modern worshippers. From the very beginning, the church acknowledged a number of texts as "apocryphal" (literally "hidden away"), meaning that they possessed special spiritual or historical merit but were not to be regarded as divine revelation. The status of some of these writings is the source of disagreement among the Protestant, Catholic, and Orthodox churches.

One important element in the writings that constitute the New Testament is the literary genre of the epistle, or letter. While the gospels are narratives concerned with the events of Jesus' life and his teaching, the letters are public communications directed at the new communities of converts (four are addressed to individuals). They were, in effect, a means of carrying on missionary activity. Hence they often employed the rhetorical style of the day and were read aloud as sermons. The letters also provided a way to respond to opponents of the Jesus movement. The theologians who decided on the canon of the New Testament perceived in the letters a timeless quality and considered them to be as essential to the formation of faith as the gospels and Acts.

Forming the core of the epistles are the thirteen "Pauline" letters, traditionally attributed to the apostle Paul (although scholars now question the attribution of some of these). The unquestionably authentic ones pre-date the gospels and hence are the earliest writings of the New Testament. Originally written in Greek, like the rest of the New Testament, they reflect Paul's mission to gentile communities and establish his authority as an apostle of Christ. His two letters to Corinth, Greece, outline his views on the doctrinal and ethical concerns of the community there. In his letter to the Galatians, a Christian community in Galatia in Asia Minor (present-day Turkey), Paul confronts the issue of whether a gentile must be circumcised before becoming a Christian. His response—no—marked a major divergence in Christian practice from that of its Jewish heritage.

The Bible is open to a wide range of interpretations
and has been used to justify opposing practices, such as
polygamy and monogamy. For many Christians, particularly those who belong to fundamentalist congregations,
the Bible is all revelation: every word is inspired by God
and hence literally true and without error. Some communities apply a more allegorical interpretation. There
are scholars who read the Bible as literature, applying
literary critical methods in their attempts to unravel the
threads of authorship, genre, and meaning.

Biblical interpretation is directly related to the
manner of translation. The vernacular or native language
Bible has a long history in Christianity. The Hebrew
Bible (the Christian Old Testament), originally written
mainly in Hebrew, was translated into Greek as early as
the third century BCE for the use of Greek-speaking
Diaspora Jews. This version, called the Septuagint, was
considered authoritative by the early church and remains
so for the Greek Orthodox church. The books of the
New Testament were originally composed in Greek.
Following the establishment of the canon, the pope
commissioned Bishop Jerome of Dalmatia (340–420CE)
to translate the Christian Bible into Latin, the language
of Western Christianity. St Jerome's work (382CE) is
called the Vulgate and was the standard Bible of Roman

Christendom until the Reformation. Today it remains the officially recognized source for Catholic translations.

By the Middle Ages, Latin ceased to be spoken by the laity and only priests and educated lay people could read the Bible. Prior to the Protestant Reformations, there were several attempts to translate the Bible, most notably that of John Wycliffe in 1382. The invention of the printing press, coupled with increased literacy, resulted in a growing demand for vernacular Bibles. At the same time, new Protestant denominations insisted that the scriptures should be accessible to all worshippers. Martin Luther's New Testament appeared in German in 1522 and a French translation of the New Testament appeared in 1582. There were a number of important English translations in the sixteenth century and in 1604 James I appointed a group of scholars to translate the Bible, now known as the King James Version. Other translated versions of the Bible enjoy wide usage, such as the English Revised Version which appeared between 1881–5 and the American Standard Version published in 1901. Today, every branch of Christianity encourages worshippers to hear and read the Bible in their native tongue, and it has been translated into more than 2,000 languages. New translations continue to reflect the variety of interpretative perspectives (see pp. 104–5).

The Lord's Prayer

❝ Our Father in heaven

hallowed be your name.

Your kingdom come.

Your will be done,

on earth as it is in heaven.

Give us this day our daily bread.

And forgive us our debts,

as we also have forgiven our debtors.

And do not bring us into temptation,

but rescue us from evil.

[For the kingdom and the power and the glory are

yours forever. Amen.] ❞

Matthew 6.9–13, from the *New Revised Standard Version Bible*. New York: Oxford University Press, 1989, p.6.

Commentary

For Christians, the most sacred text is the Bible and perhaps the most frequently spoken sacred text in Christianity is a prayer that appears in two of the four New Testament gospels—that of Matthew 6.9–13 and Luke 11.2–4. Both record Christ's answer to the question of how to pray. This text has come to be called "The Lord's Prayer" by Protestants and the "Our Father" by Roman Catholics. The term "Lord's Prayer" was not in use until the sixteenth century, and prior to that was known by its Latin name, the *Pater Noster*, or "Our Father."

The key elements of the prayer include an address, seven petitions, and a doxology. The prayer is used both in private devotions and in public worship. From earliest Christianity, the Lord's Prayer was taught to catechumens, those who were converting to Christianity. Today, it is a part of nearly all Christian liturgies or services and is used in most baptism rituals. For Roman Catholics, it is a part of the rosary, a string of beads used to count the saying of "Hail Marys."

The last clause of the prayer, "for thine is the kingdom and the power and the glory forever and ever," is a "doxology". *Doxa* in the Greek is "glory" or "praise," and has reference to royal majesty; while the rest of that word, the *logos*, means "word" or "to speak." Hence, a doxology is a short verse which praises God and typically was used as a formula for the ending of a hymn. It does not appear in the first Greek text of the New Testament into print, the *Textus Receptus*. Roman Catholics regard it as an interpolation and it is therefore omitted in the "Our Father." Although not included in the biblical passage, the prayer ends with the word "Amen," which is a Hebrew exclamation meaning "verily" and is meant to express certainty, assurance, and reality.

CHAPTER FOUR

SACRED PERSONS

All Christians, regardless of denomination, would agree that Jesus Christ is the single most holy person in Christianity. However, many Christian denominations also regard the members of the Holy Family—Mary, his mother, and Joseph, his foster-father—as sacred persons. In Roman Catholicism, Anne, his grandmother, is also held to be a holy intercessor. There are a great many other individuals considered holy or even revered by Christians. Among them are hundreds of named saints, angels, various founders of Protestant denominations as well as monastic orders, and church leaders such as bishops, cardinals, popes and theologians. It is only in Eastern Orthodoxy and Western Roman Catholicism that saints are venerated and thought to be able to provide protection and intercession for the believer.

LEFT:
Mother Teresa
(1910–1997)
dedicated her
life to helping
the poor, sick,
and dying in
India and in
1979 was
awarded the
Nobel Peace
Prize. She has
been a source
of tremendous
inspiration to
Christians the
world over.
(See also
pp.52–3.)

In Christianity, men and women who are deemed to have lived lives of extreme virtue or to have died a martyr's death are revered as "saints" (Latin, *sanctus* or *sancta*, "holy [man, woman]"). Reverence for such an individual involves cherishing his or her memory as well as venerating, and aspiring to imitate, the spirituality of a life that exemplified religious and moral ideals. Devotional practices associated with the cultivation of saints include making offerings, invocations, and vows, and petitioning for cures and miracles. The belief in the intercessory powers of saints was a cultural extension of Greco-Roman practices, in which those who had died heroic deaths were thought to exert supernatural power from their graves. The word martyr (Greek, *marturos*) means "witness" (that is, for Christ) and the women and men who went to their deaths in this period were the exemplars and heroes of early Christianity, those who had followed most closely the example of Christ. The names of the martyrs of this period, such as the women Perpetua and Felicitas (who both died in 203CE), were included in the liturgy of the early Christian communities.

Healings, exorcisms, and a variety of miracles were associated with the revering of saints' remains, and as this practice grew, from the fourth century into the Middle Ages, so also did the demand for holy relics: bones and other objects associated with the saint. Under the guidance of church leaders, Christendom thus evolved a network of sacred tombs and "reliquaries" (relic shrines). For many centuries, devotion to saints was a fundamental element of private and public Christian worship. A calendar of saints' days provided worshippers with a daily guide for meditation. Popular devotion to saints was central to medieval Christianity. To the saints' relics were added written accounts, or "hagiographies" (Greek, *hagios* or *hagia*, "saint," and *graphia*, "writing"), of their lives and miracles that encouraged devotion to the saints and portrayed their relics as instruments of divine power.

Foremost among saints in Christianity is Mary, the mother of Christ, and her husband, Joseph the carpenter. Throughout the centuries, a popular cult of veneration of Mary has grown up in both Eastern and Western strands of Christianity. "Marian" devotion developed first in the East, and can be traced to the fourth century CE. Later, the second Council of Nicaea (787CE) determined that while full adoration was reserved for God alone, Mary was due a greater degree of veneration than other saints. In Eastern Orthodoxy, special reverence for Mary is reflected in the Akathistos, a fifth-century hymn still used in worship, and in her Greek title, Theotokos ("Bearer of God"). In the Western church, the veneration

In Botticelli's Madonna of the Magnificat *(1483–5), Mary is depicted with the Christ Child and five angels. The pomegranate in her left hand symbolizes the Resurrection.*

of Mary developed much later, but remains especially vibrant in Roman Catholicism. By the twelfth century, she was commonly called simply "Our Lady" or "My Lady" (Notre Dame, Madonna) and hundreds of churches were dedicated to her. In modern times, there are many instances of Marian apparitions at places such as Lourdes, France, that have become great pilgrimage sites (see p.71). Roman Catholic devotion to Mary, like that to other saints, is based on her intercessory powers, faith in which arises from the belief that, as her son, Jesus cannot refuse his mother's pleas. While Mary does not occupy the same significant role in Protestantism, she is universally honored as the mother of Christ.

Joseph is revered as a caring husband and protector of the infant Jesus. His piety and obedience to God are essential aspects of his character. As the protector of Christ and the husband of Mary, he came to be venerated as the patron of the universal church and of fathers, carpenters, and workers. Because it is believed that he died peacefully in the company of his beloved family, he is also regarded as the patron saint of the dying.

Religious associations and communities often take a saint as their special patron, and it is customary in Roman Catholicism to name children after saints, believing that this will assure the child of the holy person's special patronage and protection. As the practice of devotion to saints expanded and developed, so too did the notion of "patron saints," still accepted in the popular devotions of Roman Catholicism and Eastern Orthodoxy. According to this idea, the lives and legends of saints, and the particular miracles attributed to them, came to be seen as evidence of specialized assistance. Thus, St. Lucy (died 304CE), who was said to have had her eyes miraculously restored after being blinded by her persecutors, became the patron of eye complaints.

Eastern Orthodox worshippers venerate far fewer saints and devotion tends to focus on the Church Fathers and the early martyrs, icons of whom are widely displayed in churches and homes. Protestant churches grant special reverence to the prophets of the Old Testament and to the apostles, but otherwise they generally regard the veneration of the saints as an idolatrous practice, and deny the intercessory powers of anyone but Christ. But both the Anglican and Lutheran churches recommend certain names for remembrance and thanksgiving.

Roman Catholicism is the only Christian denomination with a formal procedure for identifying saints and it imposes specific regulations for their cultivation. The process of adding new individuals to the official list of saints is known as "canonization." While the pope maintains the sole right to confer sainthood, a group of experts in church law at the Vatican in Rome reviews all the evidence relating to any candidate for canonization. The complex and lengthy procedure has remained largely the same for 400 years. While the veneration of saints is encouraged, neither they nor their relics may be objects of adoration, which is reserved for the persons of the Trinity (Father, Son, and Holy Spirit).

The title of saint is also applied to a number of angels—supernatural beings thought to reside in heaven and possess extraordinary powers. Angels occur frequently in the Bible, where they praise God and protect the faithful. But biblical angels, as their name (from Greek *aggelos*, "messenger") suggests, primarily act as divine messengers, intermediaries between heaven and earth; among them are the archangels ("leading angels") Gabriel, Raphael, and Michael. In the Old Testament, angels announce the births of Ishmael, Isaac, and Samson, and in the gospels they announce those of John the Baptist and Jesus, as well as proclaiming the Resurrection and advising Joseph of Nazareth in his dreams.

In the early sixth century CE, the writer Pseudo-Dionysius the Areopagite spoke of angels as part of a hierarchy of celestial forces, each with a specific cosmic function. Charged with overseeing various aspects of human affairs, angels act as rescuers, admonishers, and encouragers. The idea of the guardian angel, a protective angel assigned by God to each person, derives from scripture (Psalm 91.11). In Roman Catholicism, October 2 is a feast day for guardian angels, and on September 29 the Anglican Church celebrates the Feast of St. Michael, revered as the protector of the church against the forces of evil.

An Angelus in Praise of Mother Teresa of Calcutta

" ... At the close of this century, the panorama emerging before our eyes includes many shadows, such as the suffering and injustice oppressing individuals and peoples, the violence and the wars that ... continue to bathe so many of the earth's regions in blood. However, there are some comforting rays of light which prompt us to look at the future with hope. Our optimism is based above all on the certainty of God's constant help, which is always given to those who humbly and trustfully implore it. ... In this regard, I would like to recall the immense throng of generous people who, during the 20th century, have offered their lives to Christ by serving their brothers and sisters in humility and love. My thoughts turn in particular to Mother Teresa of Calcutta. The foundress of the Missionaries of Charity liked to say over and over: 'When we help another person, we are rewarded with peace and joy, because we have given meaning to our life.' She was a great and appreciated teacher of life, especially for young people, whom she reminded that their great task is to build peace ... May her witness be an incentive and an encouragement for many young men and women to put themselves generously at the service of the Gospel. "

From the angelus of Pope John Paul II, September 5, 1999, courtesy of the Catholic Information Network at http://www.cin.org/jp2/jp990905.html

Commentary

In this angelus, a part of the Roman Catholic mass, Pope John Paul II speaks of the inspirational activity of Mother Teresa, who in October 2003 was beatified by the pope in Rome, the penultimate step to sainthood in Roman Catholicism. She was born an Albanian Roman Catholic in a small Yugoslavian town and is said to have had an early vocation to help the poor. At the age of eighteen she joined the Irish Loreto order whose sisters operated a mission in Calcutta. She spent her life in the slums of Calcutta and in 1948 her little group of sisters was recognized as a separate order, the Missionaries of Charity.

The order has grown rapidly and is devoted to creating schools, homes for orphaned children, leprosy centers, hostels for the dying, and food kitchens for the poorest of the poor. She received the Nobel Peace Prize in 1979, saying, "I receive this in the name of the hungry, the naked, the homeless, of the crippled, of the blind, of the lepers, of all those people who feel unwanted, unloved, uncared-for throughout society, people that have become a burden to the society and are shunned by everyone." Although the Roman Catholic Church requires that the procedure for canonization begin five years after the candidate's death, the Pope waived this requirement in the case of Mother Teresa, who died in 1997.

CHAPTER FIVE

ETHICAL PRINCIPLES

All religions have moral prescriptions that provide worshippers with guidelines for what is right, good, and just. In Christianity, these injunctions have often taken the form of imperatives. For example, early Christian theologians interpreted Adam's and Eve's disobeying of God's word (Genesis 2–3) as symbolic of human inadequacy in the face of moral freedom.

Christians universally identify the Ten Commandments as an essential ethical foundation of their tradition. In addition to these moral principles are a number of other biblical injunctions for the Christian believer. Widely diverse interpretations of the same scriptural sources, reflective of differing Christian denominations and changing social contexts, have contributed to divisions within Christianity over fundamental moral questions.

LEFT: Lucas Cranach the Elder's The Fall from Grace *(1533) depicts Adam and Eve, in defiance of God's word, holding forbidden fruit plucked from the "tree of the knowledge of good and evil."*

Throughout the history of Christianity there has been little variation in the fundamental principles intended to guide believers in a Christian way of life. The authoritative biblical sources for Christian ethics are essentially the Ten Commandments, which Moses is said to have received from God on Mount Sinai (Exodus 20.2–17; Deuteronomy 5.6–21), and the teachings of Jesus. In both cases, the scriptural sources have remained relatively constant, although Roman Catholics and Lutherans on the one hand, and the Eastern Orthodox and Protestant Reformed churches on the other, differ slightly in their ordering of the Ten Commandments. The interpretation of scripture has varied within different historical, social, and geographical contexts and from one denomination to another. The same set of principles has been used, for example, to justify the maintenance of the status quo by the old Inquisition, or the promotion of a radical agenda by present-day liberation theologians (see pp.101–103).

Also crucial to the ethical foundations of Christianity is Jesus' so-called "Sermon on the Mount" (Matthew 5–7). He begins by telling the crowd that he has not come to abolish the Jewish law of Moses but to fulfill it, and warns them that anyone who breaks the commandments or teaches others to do so will be "least in the kingdom of heaven" (Matthew 5.17–20). He goes on to set out a new ethical system that extends the Mosaic law in a way that became central to the formation of a distinctly Christian morality. Jesus broadens the commandment not to kill to include even the nurturing of anger against another; expands the commandment against adultery to include lustful desires; and intensifies the injunction against taking the Lord's name in vain to include swearing by heaven, earth, or oneself.

Included in his Sermon on the Mount is a list of nine blessings for right behavior—these are referred to as "the Beatitudes" (from Latin *beatus*, "blessed") in the Western churches and as the "Commandments of Blessedness" in Eastern Orthodox churches. Unlike the Ten Commandments, the Beatitudes are not formulated as ethical imperatives. Rather, they state qualities to which Jesus' followers should aspire in order to attain blessedness and eternal life in heaven. These qualities echo the key Christian virtues of humility, simplicity, an active desire for righteousness, purity of heart, mercy, peacemaking, and a readiness to suffer persecution for the Christian faith.

The heart of the Christian ethic lies in Jesus' reevaluation of the commandments of love. Later in Matthew's gospel, when a lawyer asks him what the greatest commandment is, Jesus quotes the Old Testament: " 'You

The Church of the Beatitudes in Galilee, Israel, is located close to the Mount of Beatitudes, where Jesus is believed to have delivered his famous "Sermon on the Mount."

shall love the Lord your God with all your heart, and with all your soul, and with all your might' [Deuteronomy 6.5]. This is the greatest and first commandment. And a second is like it: 'You shall love your neighbor as yourself' [Leviticus 19.18]. On these two commandments depend all the law and the prophets." (Matthew 22.36–40; also Mark 12.29–31 and Luke 10.25–28.)

Jesus' famous parable of the Good Samaritan (Luke 10.29–37) offers his interpretation of the concept of "neighbor" as used in the commandments, and exemplifies the moral behavior that he expects from his followers. In the story, a man is robbed and left to die by the roadside. His plight is ignored by the supposedly holy men of (it is implied) the man's own nation, and he is aided by a Samaritan—an adherent of a religious tradition found in Samaria (between Judea and Galilee). Most of Jesus' hearers would have regarded Samaritans with suspicion or hostility. But in the parable, Jesus says, the Samaritan represents the true "neighbor"— someone who extends love to all from a pure heart and with no expectation of reward.

Medieval Christianity recognized "Seven Deadly [or Capital] Sins" (pride, covetousness, lust, anger, gluttony, envy, and sloth) as the source of all other sins. Pride was considered to be at the core of all vice. The seven sins were often presented in battle with their opposites— humility, generosity, chastity, meekness, temperance, fraternal love, and diligence. Prudence, temperance, fortitude, and justice are called the "Cardinal ['pivotal'] Virtues," while "faith, hope, and love" are the "Theological Virtues." The Theological Virtues constitute what Acts 9.2 calls the (Christian) "Way."

The Ten Commandments

❝ Then God spoke all these words...

'[1.] You shall have no other gods besides me.

[2.] You shall not make for yourself an idol, whether in the form of anything that is in heaven above, or that is on the earth beneath, or that is in the water ... ; you shall not bow down to them or worship them ...

[3.] You shall not make wrongful use of the name of the Lord your God, for the Lord will not acquit anyone who misuses his name.

[4.] Remember the Sabbath day, and keep it holy. Six days you shall labor and do all your work. But the seventh day is a sabbath to the Lord your God; you shall not do any work ...

[5.] Honor your father and your mother, so that your days may be long in the land that the Lord your God is giving you.

[6.] You shall not kill.

[7.] You shall not commit adultery.

[8.] You shall not steal.

[9.] You shall not bear false witness against your neighbor.

[10.] You shall not covet your neighbor's house; you shall not covet your neighbor's wife ... or anything that belongs to your neighbor.' ❞

From Exodus 20.2–17, *New Revised Standard Version Bible*. New York: Oxford University Press, 1989, p.73.

Commentary

The Ten Commandments appear in the Hebrew Bible, or Old Testament, and articulate fundamental obligations for Christians and Jews alike. Many Christians regard the ethical principles as having been divinely revealed to Moses, while others believe them to be the product of centuries of deliberation. Each commandment has generated considerable debate over the millennia—none more so than the injunction not to kill.

The question of what constitutes a just war has been an issue confronting Christianity for centuries. Referred to as the Just War Theory, it is a moral debate with religious and secular components. Two theologians—Augustine (354–430) and Thomas Aquinas (1225–1274)—are credited with formulating the basis of the theory. Certain conditions are essential in order for a war to be regarded as just. These include evidence of great injustice; proportionality between the punishment and the good to be achieved; and moral certainty that the side of justice will ultimately prevail. Aquinas claimed that war could only be declared by the authority of a sovereign leader; that those waging the war must have and exhibit rightful intentions to advance human good and welfare; and finally, that war could only be justified with the desire for peace.

CHAPTER SIX

SACRED SPACE

Christians the world over are drawn to sacred places and sites, such as the Holy Land, especially Jerusalem and Bethlehem; the Vatican, the home of the pope and sacred to Roman Catholicism; shrines which house the relics of saints; the sites of Marian apparitions; and to cemeteries and graveyards. Regardless of denomination, Christians regard the physical structure of the church as sacred space. A church, cathedral, chapel, or basilica where Christians gather to worship, listen to a preacher or celebrate a liturgy, is thought to be the "house of God." Painted images and icons, sculptures of holy persons, stained-glass windows, altars, chalices, carved altarpieces, magnificent organs, tapestries, candles, bibles, hymnals, and liturgies—all contribute to and reflect the sacred nature of church and chapel.

LEFT: The magnificent 13th-century cathedral of Notre Dame in Chartres, France. The maze laid into the floor of the nave, which has only one path to its center, represents the winding path of the soul's spiritual journey through human life.

The term "church" is used to refer to the entire body of the Christian faithful, and to any individual denomination. It also denotes the place where God is believed to reside on earth and where Christians gather for private devotion or public worship. These functions are reflected in the words for this holy space in many languages— *church*, *Kirche*, *église*, *iglesia*, and so on—which derive from either Greek *kuriakos* [*domos*] ("[house] of the Lord") or *ekklesia* ("gathering"). With an end to persecution in the fourth century CE, Christians were able to gather publicly. Under emperors such as Constantine the Great, pagan temples were torn down or converted to Christian use, and magnificent new churches were constructed, often honoring the earthly ruler as well as God. Many housed the bones of martyrs or other revered relics, unifying the early Christian landscape into a network of sacred pilgrimage sites.

The proliferation of Christian denominations today is reflected in a huge variety of architectural styles. But during the early years of Christian history, churches as distinct buildings cannot be said to have existed at all: Christians met in private homes ("house churches") for worship and gathered secretly in underground catacombs to bury their dead. The early Christians often denoted the sacred use of houses or catacombs by carved or painted symbols such as a fish (representing baptism, Christ, and the Resurrection) or a shepherd carrying a lamb (an image of pagan origin).

The earliest Christian churches in the West were in the style of the basilica (Latin, from Greek *basilike*, "royal"), the chief public building in every Roman town or city, which functioned as both a meeting hall and a law court. A basilican church has a dominating longitudinal axis leading from the main door to the chancel (or sanctuary), the area in the front (eastern) end of the church where the altar is situated. By the fifth century, every major city in Christendom possessed at least one church on the basilican plan, providing ample room for growing congregations.

In the early Middle Ages, another architectural type emerged, the cruciform church, named because its plan was in the form of the cross, with two side areas or "transepts" leading off the "nave" (Latin *navis*, literally "ship"), the long main axis. In the Eastern Orthodox church, both ancient and modern places of worship are normally constructed on a square plan and surmounted by distinctive domes.

Regardless of how humble or lavish, a Christian church is a sacred place of reverence and awe, intended to communicate Christian mysteries and the drama of salvation to its congregants. This intention is particularly apparent in the great artistic triumphs of the Romanesque (ca. 1000–1150), Gothic (ca. 1150–1550), and Baroque (ca. 1550–1750) styles of Western Christian architecture. Solid stone and exquisitely crafted or painted ornamentation, vaulted ceilings and soaring spires, and translucent light and color honored the divine and inspired the worshipper.

With an emphasis on light and uplifting space, the design of the medieval church was based on an interaction of theological symbolism and geometric harmony. The entrance was in the west, the place of the setting sun, darkness, and death, which the worshipper symbolically left behind on entering the sanctuary and approaching the altar in the east end of the church, the direction of the rising sun, light, and resurrection. The north side of the church represented the Old Testament and the south the Last Judgment and the Christian paradise on earth, the New Jerusalem.

Certain significant elements of church design have remained more or less constant, such as the altar, chancel, nave, pulpit, and (in the West) pews. The focal point of most Christian churches is the altar. Its position indicates its special role: in the early church, and to this day in Roman Catholicism, Eastern Orthodoxy, and

All churches, whether grand or simple, are considered by Christians to be sacred spaces. Here, the pastor of St. Mary Magdalene Church in the Bahamas reads from the Bible.

Anglicanism, this is where the Eucharist is celebrated. The altar is infused with a special religious mystery, and the area around it is often reserved solely for the clergy. With the establishment of the doctrine of transubstantiation (the belief, later rejected by Protestants, that the bread and wine of the Eucharist miraculously become the body and blood of Christ), the altar came to be viewed as the dwelling place of God.

In Roman Catholicism and Eastern Orthodoxy, a "tabernacle," an ornamental receptacle for the "host" (consecrated bread), is found on the main altar or on a side-altar, and in both traditions, a lamp or candles are kept burning near it. Also on the altar, during the liturgy, is an ornate chalice for serving the wine and a silver or gold paten (dish) for the bread.

The altar is normally surmounted by a crucifix and sometimes a decorated panel called an "altarpiece." In Protestant churches, the altar (frequently referred to as the Lord's Table) is usually far plainer, with just a simple cross placed on or above it. The crucifix is an image of Christ crucified on the cross; the image of the cross is that of the empty cross, emphasizing a risen Christ. In many churches, three steps mark the boundary between the sanctuary and the nave, where the congregation gathers. Anglican churches usually have a communion rail, where worshippers traditionally kneel to receive the Eucharist from the priest. In Orthodox churches the congregation is divided from the sanctuary and altar by a screen, or iconostasis ("place of images"), richly decorated with icons. Entrance to the area behind the screen is permitted only to priests.

The pulpit is an elevated stone or wooden dais used for scripture readings and sermons. In Protestant churches, where the reading of scripture is central to the service, the pulpit may be in a very prominent position. Pews were a medieval innovation in the West: for many centuries, Christians stood during the liturgy, as is still the case in the majority of Eastern Orthodox churches.

While most Christian places of worship are called churches, other terms are also used. Historically, a "cathedral" (short for "cathedral church") housed the *cathedra*, the official seat or throne of the local bishop. A small, subsidiary, or private church or worship space is often called a chapel (Latin *cappella*, literally "little cloak"—the word derives from a famous medieval shrine near Tours, France, containing the cloak of St. Martin). A chapel may be to one side of the main nave or chancel of a larger church, within a private institution such as a school, hospital, or even an airport, or within a royal or aristocratic residence. Many Protestant denominations employ the term to denote their principal places of worship.

Throughout their history, Christian places of worship have been adorned with images representing sacred stories and mysteries, expressed in stone and wooden sculptures, intricate mosaics, frescoes, painted and carved altarpieces, and stained or painted glass. For the illiterate mass of medieval worshippers, religious images served a didactic purpose as well as being aids to spiritual awareness and contemplation.

Among the remarkable architectural achievements of the Romanesque and Gothic cathedrals of western

Europe was the development of the medium of stained (colored) glass, suffusing the internal space with light and color. Stained-glass windows may record biblical or saintly portraits or narratives, or they may be more geometrical and abstract in design. The shape and proportions of some windows, such as the "rose" windows of Chartres cathedral, France (see illustration, p.62), may possess sacred numerological significance—for example, groups of three represent the Trinity, of four the gospels, and so on. The concept of the church as the house of God led in medieval times to the idea that the physical fabric of the building represented the Virgin Mary, the vessel in which God became incarnate.

Some Christians at various periods have been strongly opposed to the veneration of images in churches, at times seeking to remove them (usually with the exception of the cross) on the grounds that they breach the biblical commandment against idolatry (Exodus 20.4). In the eighth century, the iconoclasts ("image-breakers") of the Eastern church succeeded in officially banning all icons for several decades, and the more radical Protestants of the sixteenth and seventeenth centuries stripped many churches of their decoration. The austere grandeur of many medieval cathedrals in Protestant Europe today is usually the result of such action; in the Middle Ages they would probably have been places of breathtaking color from frescoes and stained-glass windows.

In the Holy Land, many churches, such as those in Bethlehem or Galilee, mark sites connected with the life of Christ. Every year, thousands of Christian pilgrims visit these places. There are numerous other Christian pilgrimage sites outside the Holy Land, most associated with the relics of saints, which are revered for the sacred power they are believed to possess. Pilgrimages are primarily intended as acts of devotion, to ask or thank a saint for intercession, or as penance. Among the most famous pilgrimage sites are Santiago de Compostela, Spain (home of the reputed relics of St. James the Apostle), and Canterbury cathedral, England (which houses the tomb of St. Thomas à Becket, an archbishop of Canterbury murdered in 1170). Many pilgrimage centers have arisen around sites of visions of the Virgin Mary. Some of the most notable are at Fatima (Portugal), Lourdes (France), and Czestochowa (Poland). Lourdes, perhaps the best known, is where in 1858, a peasant girl claimed to have had visions of Mary at a grotto where a spring appeared that has since been regarded as a source of miraculous cure. Each year thousands of the faithful flock to the Church of the Rosary built above the grotto.

Empress Helena's Churches at Bethlehem

" The Empress Helena dedicated two churches to the God whom she adored, one at the grotto which had been the scene of the Saviour's birth; the other on the mount of his ascension. For he who was "God with us" had submitted to be born even in a cave of the earth, and the place of his nativity was called Bethlehem by the Hebrews. Accordingly, the pious empress honored with rare memorials the scene of her travail he who bore this heavenly child, and beautified the sacred cave with all possible splendor. The emperor himself soon after testified his reverence for the spot by princely offerings. ... And farther, Empress Helena raised a stately structure on the Mount of Olives, in memory of his ascent to heaven, ... erecting a sacred church and temple on the very summit of the mount. And indeed authentic history informs us that in this very cave the Saviour imparted his secret revelations to his disciples. ... Thus did Helena Augusta, the pious mother of a pious emperor, erect over the two ... caverns two noble and beautiful monuments of devotion, worthy of ever-lasting remembrance, to the honor of God her Saviour. "

From *Eusebius: Church history, Life of Constantine the Great, and Oration in praise of Constantine* by Ernest Cushing Richardson (The Bagster translation, 1890) in *A select library of Nicene and Post-Nicene Fathers*, Volume 1, edited by H. Wace and P. Schaff. Reprinted by Wm Erdmans: Grand Rapids, Michigan, 1986, p.162.

Commentary

Eusebius (ca. 260–ca. 339CE), the author of this excerpt, was the bishop of Caesarea and the first historian of Christianity. In 313CE, Emperor Constantine proclaimed toleration for Christianity and began his patronage of the faith. Empress Helena, Constantine's mother, had a major role to play in Christian history due to her discovery of what she believed to be the true cross and to her building of churches in Bethlehem and Jerusalem. This passage refers to the two basilicas, or churches, she built in Bethlehem in commemoration of the major events in Christ's life.

The Church of the Nativity is structured octagonally at the eastern end, built around the cave where it was believed that Jesus was born. The octagon is called a *martyrion*, a Greek term referring to a shrine built to witness a place associated with the life of Jesus, the Virgin Mary, or any other saint. *Martyria* are found in all parts of the early Christian world. They were usually constructed under imperial patronage.

The second church referred to is a small basilica at Mamre, near Hebron, on the Mount of Olives. Helena is also credited with having built the *martyrion* basilica at the Church of the Holy Sepulchre in Jerusalem. Today these churches are venerated as pilgrimage sites.

CHAPTER SEVEN

SACRED TIME

Sacred time in the Christian tradition marks remembrances of holy persons and events through festivals, celebrations, and liturgies. It is a cyclical calendar that integrates theology and ancient agricultural events with pre-Christian celebrations. The rituals which mark these sacred times and celebrate holy persons vary widely across the tradition, but in the medieval world the Christian calendar permeated the rhythm of life for everyone, tolling the hour of the day and informing the worshipper when to fast and when to feast. Today, Catholic and Orthodox Christians follow an intricately structured pattern of ritual life; evangelical Christians, however, emphasize the two poles of the religious calendar, Christmas and Easter. But for all Christians, the liturgical calendar affects how they worship and pray.

LEFT: An Ethiopian procession in the Old City, Jerusalem, on Palm Sunday, the Sunday before Easter and the first day of Holy Week. The event celebrates Jesus' triumphal entry into Jerusalem, when people are believed to have scattered palm leaves on the road before him.

Christians observe a liturgical calendar, or yearly cycle of holy days, that moves between two principal festivals central to all branches of Christianity: Christmas, a celebration of the nativity, or birth, of Jesus, and Easter, which celebrates his salvific resurrection.

The New Testament provides few clues as to the actual time of Jesus' birth, although it has been noted that in Palestine shepherds would have watched their flocks in the hills during the nighttime in summer rather than in winter. In the Roman empire, the winter solstice was observed on December 25 as the celebration of the "Invincible Sun" (Sol Invictus), and this was also the time of Saturnalia, an exuberant and popular Roman festival. In the late fourth century, with Rome's abolition of pagan festivals, the date of Sol Invictus was adopted as the birthday of Jesus, who is hailed as the "light of the world" in the gospels (John 8.12).

Taking December 25 as a starting point, the church authorities were able to calculate several other significant Christian celebrations, such as the Annunciation (Luke 1.26–38), which was demed to have taken place exactly nine months earlier on March 25; the Circumcision (Luke 2.21) on January 1 (which would have taken place within eight days of Jesus' birth, in accordance with Jewish law); and the Epiphany, or Theophany, marking the homage of the eastern wise men to the messiah (Matthew 2), on January 6.

Amid all the festivities that now surround Christmas, it is easy to forget that Easter, the commemoration of Jesus' redeeming death and resurrection, is the church's holiest festival. As an observant Jew, Jesus went to Jerusalem to celebrate the Passover, or Pesach—whence the name for Easter in many churches (via Greek and Latin *Pascha*). Matthew, Mark, and Luke describe his final meal with his disciples, the "Last Supper," as a Passover meal, after which he was arrested, tried, and condemned. Jesus was executed on the following day, marked by Christians as "Good Friday" and the faith's most solemn festival. He died within a few hours and because of the approaching Sabbath (Friday evening to Saturday evening) he was entombed in haste.

According to the gospels, a group of women found the tomb empty on the following Sunday; a divine messenger proclaimed to them that Jesus had been raised from the dead. The Resurrection is commemorated on Easter Sunday, the most joyous day in the Christian calendar. Many early Christians celebrated the occasion at Passover (which falls on the fourteenth day of the Jewish month of Nisan, the time of the spring equinox), but the church later fixed upon the Sunday following the first full moon after the equinox.

Young girls holding candles at a Swedish church in Pennsylvania on the feast day of Lucia (December 13). The event is celebrated throughout Sweden as a festival of lights.

The week preceding Easter Sunday is known as Holy Week and begins with Palm Sunday, which marks Jesus' entry into Jerusalem on a donkey, when people scattered branches (of palm, according to John 12.13) before him. In Eastern Orthodoxy and Roman Catholicism it includes the liturgies of Maundy Thursday (marking the Last Supper and Christ's washing of the feet of his disciples [John 13]); Good Friday (the Crucifixion and the end of Lent); Holy Saturday (the resting of Christ's body in the tomb); and "Paschal Vigil," in which worshippers await the arrival of Easter Sunday at midnight.

Christmas and Easter are preceded by two seasons of special holiness, Advent and Lent respectively. Advent (Latin *adventus*, "arrival") anticipates both the celebration of Jesus' birth and also his expected Second Coming. In Western traditions, it takes in the four Sundays preceding December 25, while in Eastern Orthodoxy it is the forty days before Christmas. However, all churches recognize the first Sunday of Advent as the beginning of the liturgical year. Advent calendars are a traditional and popular way of teaching chidren to count the twenty-five days until Christmas.

Easter is preceded by Lent (an old English word for "springtime"), a forty-day preparatory period of repentance, fasting, and self-denial that begins on "Ash Wednesday." The days immediately before Lent are commonly marked by a final round of merrymaking that ends on "Shrove Tuesday" or "Mardi Gras" (French, "Fat Tuesday"), traditionally the last time one was permitted to eat meat before Easter, hence the term "carnival" (Italian *carne*, "meat").

After Easter comes Pentecost (Greek *pentekoste*, "fiftieth [day]"), or Whitsunday, commemorating the descent of the Holy Spirit to Jesus' disciples (Acts 2.1–4). In the New Testament account, this event was marked by *glossolalia* ("speaking in tongues"), a phenomenon characterizing present-day Pentecostalism. In Eastern Christianity, two other holy days are of vital importance: the Feast of the Transfiguration (August 6), which recalls Jesus' appearance in glory with Moses and Elijah (Matthew 17.1–13; Mark 9.2–13; Luke 9.28–36), and the Feast of the Assumption of Mary (August 15), which commemorates her being taken ("assumed"), body and soul, into heaven.

Over the centuries, local saints' festivals and other regional feasts, such as the dedication of a church, brought considerable variation and confusion into the liturgical calendar. In 1582, Pope Gregory XIII systematized the holy days for the Roman Catholic church as part of a general reform of the Julian calendar, which had gradually fallen out of step with the solar year by twelve days since being established by Julius Caesar in Roman times. Protestant churches eliminated the majority of these feasts, regarding them as having no foundation in the Bible, but by the mid-eighteenth century most of the churches and states of western Europe, both Catholic and

Protestant, had adopted Gregory's adjustment to the old Julian calendar. Retained in some liturgical calendars are festivals focused on individual and regional saints such as St. Patrick, patron saint of Ireland (March 17), and St. David, patron saint of Wales (March 1).

The majority of Orthodox countries adopted the Gregorian calendar for secular use, but the Orthodox church has continued to observe the old Julian calendar. Hence there is an enduring discrepancy with regard to the dates of Easter and Christmas between Roman Catholics and Protestants on the one hand, and the Eastern Orthodox church on the other. For example, December 25 in the Julian calendar falls on January 6 in the Gregorian calendar, while the different Orthodox date for the spring equinox similarly affects the timing of the Orthodox Easter.

In Christian tradition, the word "liturgy" has two distinct applications. Generally speaking, it applies to all communal church services, in contrast to a wide array of private devotions. The term also refers to a specific ritual event, which for Roman Catholics and Eastern Orthodox worshippers is synonymous with the celebration of the Eucharist (Holy Communion or Lord's Supper) and for Protestant denominations is called the "Liturgy of the Word" and denotes the celebration of scripture. The term "liturgy" itself (Greek *leitourgia*, "work of the people") connotes the highly congregational aspect of much Christian worship, in which the faithful gather to participate in the liturgy by speaking, singing, or praying in unison.

Christianity has numerous rituals that are designed to recall and honor the life of Christ and bring the worshipper into direct proximity with the sacred. These sacred rites or orders of worship also reflect sacred time in Christian traditions, in that they are thought to occur in *illo tempore*, "in that time." Included in these rituals are the sacraments; the reading of the Bible; prescribed prayers; vigils; fasts; and pilgrimages (see p.71). For many monks, nuns, and priests, daily ritual includes an obligation to chant the "Divine Office," which involves a series of communal acts of daily worship called "hours"—lauds, prime, terce, sext, none, vespers, compline, and matins. Otherwise, churches may sometimes observe daily matins (morning service) and "vespers" or "evensong" (evening service).

Central to Christian ritual is the celebration of sacred acts known as "sacraments." Most Christians would agree that Christ himself instituted two sacraments, that of baptism (a ritual of initiation into the body of the faithful that also usually involves naming) and that of the Eucharist, or Lord's Supper, a ritual remembrance of the Passion. Both these sacraments have been the focus of intense disagreement and today account for some of the major differences between denominations. Baptism, which involves immersion in or pouring on of water, is a ritual which in several denominations initiates infants into the religion and is accompanied by the naming of the child. For other Christians, it is reserved exclusively for adults.

The meaning and significance of the Eucharist (Greek *eucharistia*, "thanksgiving"), for many the foundational sacrament of Christianity, have also been a source of great controversy. For Roman Catholic, Eastern Orthodox, and some Anglican worshippers, the bread ("host") and wine that are given to believers are thought to be literally transformed into the body and blood of Christ through the act of consecration by the priest. This mystery of faith is known as "transubstantiation." Lutherans accept a modified notion called "consubstantiation," meaning that the substances of bread and wine coexist with the body and blood. Calvinists and many Anglicans believe that there is no physical change in the bread and wine but that they convey to the worshipper the power of the body and blood (a notion called "virtualism"). Most other Protestant denominations believe that the Eucharist is purely a memorial rite and that there is no transformation of the bread and wine.

In Roman Catholicism and Eastern Orthodoxy, only the baptized may partake of the Eucharist. In these churches, five other sacraments are also held to bring divine power into the life of the believer. These are confirmation (a renewal of baptism with holy oil); penance (confession and absolution); marriage; ordination (investment with priestly powers); and extreme unction (anointing of the sick and dying). For worshippers in these traditions, the liturgical rites not only mark out the lifespan of the believer, they are also held to be necessary for salvation. In most Protestant denominations, both baptism and the Eucharist are considered obligatory due to scriptural authority, but are not essential for salvation. For all denominations, baptism marks the beginning of one's life as a Christian.

By the second century CE, the Christian Sabbath, or the "Lord's Day" (Revelation 1.10), had moved to the first day of the week (Sunday) rather than the last (Saturday), not only to distinguish it from the Jewish Sabbath but also, and principally, because this was the day on which Jesus' resurrection occurred. On Sundays, therefore, Christians regularly gather together to re-create or remember the Lord's Supper. Rituals that are associated with the

Lord's Day primarily remember and celebrate what Christians regard as Christ's sacrifice of body and blood.

The following gospel passage (Luke 22.19–20), often spoken by a priest or minister, is incorporated into most Christian rituals celebrating the Eucharist: "And he took bread, and when he had given thanks he broke it and gave it to them, saying: 'This is my body which is given for you; do this in remembrance of me.' And likewise he took the cup after supper, saying, 'This cup which is poured out for you is the new covenant in my blood.'" Sunday services in all traditions are the essential element of the liturgical year.

Liturgical observances, such as the celebration of sacraments and the sabbath, are the traditional rituals of Christian worship. In addition, there is a wide range of non-liturgical rituals, often unstructured and spontaneous, such as private prayer. Because these personal rituals form a significant part of the ritual life of many Christians, they also mark sacred time. For Eastern Orthodoxy this would include devotion to icons, which occupy a special place even in the home, where a lamp, candle, or incense is burned before the icon during prayer. It is also a common practice in Roman Catholicism to light candles and pray in churches and at home outside service times.

The Libretto from Handel's "Messiah"

" 'Look, the virgin shall conceive, and bear a son, and
they shall name him Emmanuel.'[God is with us.} ...

'The people who walked in darkness have seen a
great light: those who lived in a land of deep darkness—
on them light has shined.' ...

'For a child has been born for us, a son given to us;
authority rests upon his shoulders; and he is named
Wonderful Counselor, Mighty God, Everlasting Father,
Prince of Peace.' ...

'In that region there were shepherds living in the
fields, keeping watch over their flock by night. Then an
angel of the Lord stood before them, and the glory of the
Lord shone round about them, and they were terrified.
But the angel said to them, "Do not be afraid; for see—
I am bringing you good news of great joy for all the
people: to you is born this day in the city of David
a Saviour, who is the Messiah, the Lord. This will be
a sign for you: you will find a child wrapped in bands
of cloth and lying in a manger." And suddenly there
was with the angel a multitude of the heavenly host,
praising God and saying, 'Glory to God in the highest
heaven, and on earth peace, good will among people.' **"**

From Matthew 1.23; Isaiah 9.2; Isaiah 9.6; and Luke 2.8–14, *New Revised Standard Version Bible*. Oxford
University Press: New York, 1989, p.2, pp.706–707, p.707, and pp.59–60.

Commentary

George Frideric Handel completed the oratorio, which he called "Messiah," in just twenty-four days during 1741. It was first performed for Easter, on April 13, 1742, in Dublin, Ireland. When it was performed in London a year later, King George II sprang to his feet during the singing of the Hallelujah Chorus. It has since been customary for everyone to stand during this portion of the concert.

The libretto, written by Charles Jennens, comprises passages from the Old and New Testaments, drawn from the King James Version of the Bible. Performed in full, the oratorio lasts four hours and is divided into three parts. Part I is devoted to prophecy and the coming of the messiah; Part II is concerned with the redemption of humankind and the sacrifice of Jesus; and Part III is dedicated to Christian thanksgiving for the defeat of death.

Beginning with the story of the nativity and moving through the Passion and Crucifixion, the "Messiah" celebrates the Christian liturgical year through the singing of biblical passages. While it was originally intended as a piece of sacred music focused on issues of doctrine and faith for the Lenten season, today the work is one of the most famous pieces of English sacred music and is widely venerated as a Christmas tradition.

CHAPTER EIGHT

DEATH AND THE AFTERLIFE

At the heart of Christianity lies the belief in an eternal life after death. This belief is founded on God's redemptive activity to save sinful humankind and is manifested in the incarnation and resurrection of Christ and extended to all believers. As with other essential elements of Christianity, worshippers find authority for the doctrine of immortality in the Bible. One of the most quoted passages is John 3.16: "For God so loved the world that he gave his only Son, so that everyone who believes in him may not perish but may have eternal life." Ritual acknowledgment of the belief in eternal life is apparent in Christian burial practices and is included in a number of Christian liturgies through the recitation of the creed. The last line of all Christian creeds affirms the worshipper's faith in the resurrection of the body and "life everlasting."

LEFT:
A statue representing the passion ("suffering"), death, and resurrection of Christ is paraded on a float during a Holy Week procession in Seville, Spain. Christian belief in the immortality of the soul is based, in part, on Christ's resurrection.

Christians have always made a distinction between the body and the soul, affirming the ability of the soul to survive the catastrophe of death. Beliefs in the immortality of the soul are linked to ideas about resurrection, both individual and eschatological (referring to "last things" [Greek, *eskhatos*, "last" and *logos*, "word"]). Christian tradition teaches that with the Second Coming of Christ there will be a final judgment of the living and the dead, and that this will complete creation by the opening of the kingdom of heaven.

Salvation, the term for the state of redemption and reconciliation with God, is a primary spiritual goal of Christians. Interpretations of the nature of and path to salvation vary, but the view that humans have an immortal soul is generally accepted in Christianity. Aside from the Calvinist notion of predestination, which holds that only an elect body of worshippers is saved, in most Protestant communities salvation is guaranteed solely by the worshipper's faith, the acceptance of Jesus Christ.

While distinctions exist among Christians about what qualifies one for salvation or damnation, it is a tradition of all denominations that the saved will spend eternity rewarded in the paradise of heaven while the damned will be punished forever in hell. The precise location of the everlasting life is a complex issue for theologians and worshippers alike. In the Middle Ages, Christians envisaged four possible locations for the soul after death: heaven, hell, purgatory, or limbo. In the Old Testament, the term "heaven" refers to the blue firmament, the region above the clouds where God resides, and the New Testament repeatedly refers to the "kingdom of heaven" or the "kingdom of God" (terms that encompass various other meanings) as a place where believers are gloriously present with God. For Christians today, heaven is conceptualized as a state of triumphant glory and joy, a blissful paradise in the presence of the beatific vision of God.

Enmity with God leads to the state of damnation in hell. Throughout Christian history, hell has been envisioned as a place of unspeakable punishment, an eternal inferno, presided over by the Devil, or Satan. The damned are eternally estranged from God; hence their abode is said to be as remote as possible from heaven, located in a fiery darkness.

For medieval Christians, purgatory (from Latin *purgare*, "to purge, make clean") was the place where souls that were neither damned nor free of sin would suffer for a time after death and be cleansed of their sins. This belief was founded on the notion that sin and God cannot coexist and consequently the soul must become sinless

A 13th-century enamel panel from the Verdun Altar in Klosterneuburg abbey, Vienna, depicting the resurrection of the dead (in Latin, below, "The Dead Arise").

in order to enter into the eternal heavenly paradise. In modern Roman Catholic teaching, purgatory is a state or condition of punishment for those whose souls at death are not free of sin or whose sins have not been remitted by God through the sacrament of penance. Protestant reformers rejected the belief in purgatory as without biblical foundation. Some Roman Catholic theologians still regard limbo, a peaceful state, but without the possibility of the presence of God, as the destination for unbaptized infants.

The traditional manner of caring for the dead in Christianity is burial. Customs vary historically and include a wide range of regional differences. Burial practices are an expression of Christian belief in immortality. As with other religious traditions, disposal of the deceased is a rite of passage, leaving one world for another. Care of the dead requires ceremonial rituals. The body is prepared and displayed for farewell followed by burial or cremation. Funeral services and traditional wakes have a comforting aspect and are often concluded with a common meal shared by the mourners.

Many denominations commemorate the dead in special masses, prayers, and festivals. The dates of such feasts vary: in Greek Orthodoxy, the dead are remembered on the eve of Sexagesima (the second Sunday before Lent) or on the eve of Pentecost, while the equivalent Armenian Orthodox feast falls on Easter Monday. The Roman Catholic festival, All Souls' Day (November 2), has its origin in the medieval cult of the dead and in the Middle Ages, together with All Saints' Day (November 1), it ranked only after Christmas and Easter in importance. It is a highly charged holy day in many countries, a time to pray for and remember the departed.

The Committal of the Deceased

66 *The priest metyng the Corps at the Churche style, shalt say:*
'I am the resurreccion and the life (sayth the Lord): he
that beleveth in me, yea though he were dead, yet shall
he live. And whosoever lyveth and beleveth in me:
shall not dye for ever.' ...
'We brought nothyng into this worlde, neyther may we
carye any thyng out of this worlde. The Lord geveth,
and the Lord taketh awaie. Even as it pleaseth the
Lorde, so cummeth thynges to passe: blessed be the
name of the Lorde.' ... 99

[More prayers are said or sung until the corpse is ready
to be laid in the ground.]

66 *Then the priest castyng earth upon the Corps, shall saye:*
'I commende thy soule to God the father almighty,
and thy body to the grounde, earth to earth, asshes
to asshes, dust to dust, in sure and certayne hope
of resurreccion to eternall lyfe, through our Lord Jesus
Christ, who shall chaunge our vile body, that it
may be lyke to his glorious body, accordyng to the
myghtie workyng wherby he is hable to subdue all
thynges to himselfe.' ... 99

From *The First and Second Prayer Books of Edward VI* [*Book of Common Prayer*]. Introduced by Edgar C. S.
Gibson. J.M. Dent and E.P. Dutton: London and New York, 1910.

Commentary

Belief in an afterlife is an essential part of Christian faith, as evident in most funeral services. The well-known phrase uttered at funerals, "ashes to ashes, dust to dust" does not appear in the Bible, only in the Anglican or Episcopalian *Book of Common Prayer*. This collection of services and rituals in the vernacular first appeared in 1549 and has had an enormous impact on Christian religious life; although extensively revised since, much of the original and its second edition of 1552 remains recognizable—such as the "Order for the Burial of the Dead."

The service suggests that it is customary for the celebrant to meet the coffin at the entrance to the church or chapel and to go before it inside, accompanied by anthems said or sung, and similarly when the procession moves out to the cemetery. A church service follows and includes hymns, scriptural readings, prayers, an address, and testimonials. Although most denominations now permit cremation, the traditional form of Christian funeral was the burial. The committal portion of the service was the lowering of the casket into the grave or, in some cases, the casting of earth onto the casket. It was at this moment that the celebrant enunciated "ashes to ashes, dust to dust," a phrase based on similar words used in Genesis 3.19: "... you are dust, and to dust you shall return."

CHAPTER NINE

SOCIETY AND RELIGION

While faith is uniquely personal, the practice of Christianity is largely a group phenomenon, involving dynamic interaction with society, both on a local and a global scale. Throughout its history, Christianity has influenced and reinforced society's norms and values, both challenging and reflecting cultural mores. The scientific and political questions of the modern world have presented increasingly difficult ethical dilemmas for Christians, reflecting the complex relationship of church, state, and society. The question of resistance to an immoral government, bioethical decisions, ecological concerns, the use of military technology, capital punishment, and the treatment of refugees from war-torn states—all of these issues, and many others, are debated by Christian churches, their clergy and their congregations.

LEFT: Civil rights activist, theologian, and preacher, Martin Luther King Jr. (1929–1968) was the most prominent Christian figure in the civil rights movement of the 1950s and 1960s. His impassioned mission to secure equal rights for blacks was strongly informed by the Christian faith.

The Bible calls upon Christians to obey the laws of the state, notably in Jesus' instruction to "give to the emperor the things that are the emperor's, and to God the things that are God's" (Mark 12.17). However, the relationship between the ecclesiastical and secular authorities has varied at different times and in different countries. The later Roman emperors played a vital role in church affairs, convening councils, prosecuting heretics, and determining church leadership. These functions were inherited in the East by the Byzantine emperors and in the West by the rulers of the Holy Roman empire (a confederation of central European states originally founded by Charlemagne in 800CE and abolished by Napoleon in 1804).

In the Middle Ages, the political power of the clergy increased, especially in the West, following the twelfth-century "Investiture Controversy"—a dispute over the extent of the authority sovereigns could exercise in ecclesiastical affairs—from which the church emerged with sole authority over spiritual matters. The six-teenth-century Protestant Reformations saw a further entrenchment of the principle of the separation of church and state. In Protestant countries, all legal and political authority came to lie with secular leaders (except in England, however, where the monarch is seen as the "supreme governor" of the Church of England).

In recent centuries and in the modern era, anticlerical and anti-ecclesiastical movements have arisen owing largely to criticisms of ecclesiastical wealth and the perceived abuse of clerical privilege. In the twentieth century, several governments, including those of France, Mexico, and Spain, have pursued expressly anticlerical policies, placing restrictions on the clergy and taking over church property. In Communist states, anticlericalism has been pursued as part of a general anti-religious ideology extending to the prohibition of the public practice of the religion.

While all Christian denominations claim a status distinct from the state, many Christians are keenly interested in engaging in society and actively pursuing social change. Modern Christian thinking includes a number of radical approaches that rethink theological foundations in terms of the poor and oppressed, and maintain that theology, by its nature—especially its concern with God's relationship to humanity—has practical and political implications.

As Christianity entered the twentieth century, several Christian thinkers and activists brought a challenging social vision to their faith. Protestants and Catholics alike argued passionately—as do today's liberation and feminist theologians—that Christianity has an obligation to engage with social problems, to speak out against violations of human rights.

The notion of a "social gospel" was founded on the belief that humanity suffers from problems only religion can resolve. Social gospel movements such as the Salvation Army, established in Britain in 1878 by William Booth (1829–1912), worked to establish hospitals, orphanages, homeless shelters, and soup kitchens as well

A mother and child receive help from a clinic in Mali staffed by nuns. Many religious orders devote a great deal of time and effort to humanitarian assistance in the developing world.

as employing overtly political strategies aimed at economic justice and racial equality. The Salvation Army is particularly evangelical in its rescue work, but most Christian social movements today are less concerned with the salvation of those they help than with their physical and social well-being. Movements that subscribe to the idea of the social gospel are often challenged by conservative and fundamentalist groups primarily concerned with evangelizing and with maintaining traditional Christian values.

The term "liberation theologies" embraces a variety of radical Christian strands, including liberation theology proper and feminist theology. Liberation theology, which originated among Catholics in Latin America, looks for radical social change to eliminate poverty and portrays Jesus as the chief liberator of the oppressed. Liberation theology's advocates hold that suffering humanity constitutes God's elect, and they highlight the books of Exodus (the account of one nation's liberation) and Job (the story of an innocent individual's suffering). Some Roman Catholic leaders have criticized liberation theology, maintaining that, because it incorporates Marxist theory, it reduces faith to politics. However, it might be observed that there has been a long tradition of Christian political engagement, even in Catholic countries—as exemplified by the Christian socialist and Christian democratic movements of Italy, Germany, and elsewhere.

Feminist theology is founded on the belief that traditional theology is fundamentally patriarchal. The primary goal of feminist theologians is the elimination of oppression based on gender, race, or class, and the promotion of a full humanity for all Christians. In seeking to address a perceived systematic oppression of women in Christian history, theology, and practice, feminist theologians use scripture and tradition in their critique of patriarchal theology and their quest to recover the lost experiences of women. Female ordination is a major issue dividing the main denominations: most Protestant churches now have women priests, while Roman Catholicism and Orthodoxy remain firmly opposed.

Bitter disagreements have continued to pit Christian groups against one another. Many interdenominational conflicts date back to the Reformation or, like the Roman Catholic-Orthodox clash in the former Yugoslavia, even further. The policies of segregation in the southern United States and of apartheid in South Africa both found support from local denominations in those regions but met with fierce opposition from churches outside.

Since the sixteenth and seventeenth centuries, science has called fundamental Christian teachings into question and continues to raise new doctrinal, moral, and ethical issues. Creationism and evolution still split believers after almost a century and a half, to which must now be added bioethical debates on questions such as cloning and genetic engineering. (See also p.61 for a discussion of "Just War.")

Other issues facing Christians include environmentalism versus material development; the use of capital punishment; abortion; and the complex questions of sexuality and the family. While Protestant churches do not regard marriage as a sacramental bond, unlike the Roman Catholic and Eastern Orthodox churches, all Christians liken the institution of marriage to the relationship of the church and Christ (see Ephesians 5.22–33). Historically, the church has regarded the family as vital for the transmission of Christian values, and both progressive and conservative theologians uphold the social importance of marriage and the family. However, there is wide disagreement over the laws that govern marriage, sexuality, and the raising of families. Controversies over issues such as the equality of marriage partners, family planning, and sexual orientation, show little sign of ending their tendency to divide the faithful.

Genesis and *The Woman's Bible*

66 Here is the sacred historian's first account of the advent
of woman; a simultaneous creation of both sexes, in the
image of God. It is evident ... that there was consultation
in the Godhead, and that the masculine and feminine
elements were equally represented. ...

But [in the doctrine of the trinity] instead of three
male personages ... a Heavenly Father, Mother, and Son
would seem more rational. ... If language has any
meaning, we have in these texts a plain declaration of
the existence of the feminine element in the Godhead,
equal in power and glory with the masculine. ...

Thus Scripture, as well as science and philosophy,
declares the eternity and equality of sex the philosophical
fact, without which there could have been no perpetua-
tion of creation, ... no awakening nor progressing in
the world of thought.

The masculine and feminine elements ... are as
essential to the maintenance of the equilibrium of the
universe as positive and negative electricity, ... [as] the
laws of attraction which bind together all we know of
this planet whereon we dwell. 99

From a discussion of Genesis 1.26–28 in *The Woman's Bible*, by Elizabeth Cady Stanton (Foreword by
Maureen Fitzgerald). Northeastern University Press: Boston, 1993, pp.14–15.

Commentary

The author of this biblical commentary on Genesis 1.26–28 ("And God said, Let us make man in our image" ...) from *The Woman's Bible* is Elizabeth Cady Stanton who was both a leading activist for women's rights and a pioneering biblical scholar. She was born in Johnstown, New York, on November 12, 1815, the daughter of a judge. From an early age she developed an interest in the laws that discriminated against women.

In 1895 she was a member of the revising committee that worked on *The Woman's Bible*, offering a full commentary on both the New Testament and the Old Testament. Stanton and her feminist colleagues intended the commentary as an interpretation to correct Biblical exegesis, which they believed to be unfairly biased against women. After a brief introduction by Stanton, this is the first biblical citation to receive commentary, most likely because of the reference to the creation of man and woman. It should be noted that *The Woman's Bible* used Julie Smith's 1888 translation of the Bible.

The Woman's Bible is regarded as the first feminist commentary on the Bible. While it is still cited by modern scholars as a pioneering work, in its time, Stanton's interpretation encountered considerable criticism from the Christian churches.

GLOSSARY

apocrypha sacred writings not univerasally regarded as part of the canon of scripture.

Bible Christianity's most sacred text, divided into two parts: the Old Testament (or Hebrew Bible), containing thirty-nine books, and the New Testament, containing twenty-seven books.

Christ a Greek translation (*christos*) of the Hebrew word *mashiach* ("messiah" or "anointed one"), the figure who was sent by God to herald the end of the present world and the beginning of the divine kingdom.

Church Fathers male theologians of the early Christian centuries (ca. 200–500CE) who helped shape Christian doctrine.

Eucharist (also known as Holy Communion and Lord's Supper) a sacrament which commemorates the Last Supper, when Jesus took bread and wine, saying respectively: "This is my body" and "this is my blood." The meaning of the Eucharist has provoked great debate. But for many, the bread ("host") and wine given to believers is thought to be transformed into the body and blood of Christ through consecration by a priest.

evangelicalism a movement whose adherents believe themselves to be "born again."

gospels the first four books of the New Testament, written by Matthew, Mark, Luke, and John (the "evangelists"), which focus on Jesus' life and teaching. "Gospel" is a direct translation of the Greek *euangelion*, "good news."

Holy Spirit the third person of the **Trinity**. The Spirit was believed to have been involved at key moments in Jesus' earthly existence. The Acts of the Apostles makes numerous references to healing, prophecy, exorcism, and speaking in tongues, all of which are associated with the activities of the Spirit.

liberation theologies a number of radical Christian strands whose adherents regard Jesus as the liberator of the oppressed and mobilize for social change to eradicate poverty and discrimination.

Marian of or pertaining to Mary, mother of **Christ**.

Pentateuch the first five books of the Old Testament.

Septuagint the Greek translation of the Hebrew Bible, so called because it was supposedly undertaken by seventy (Latin, *septuaginta*, "seventy") scholars in Alexandria, Egypt.

sacrament a sacred act believed to confer divine grace.

Trinity a central doctrine of Christianity which holds that there is one God, but that he comprises three persons—Father, Son, and Holy Spirit—worshipped as a single entity.

GENERAL BIBLIOGRAPHY

Brown, Peter. *The Rise of Western Christendom: Triumph and Diversity,
200–1000AD*. Oxford: Blackwell, 1997.

Brown, Schuyler. *The Origins of Christianity: A Historical Introduction to the
New Testament*. Rev. ed. New York: Oxford University Press, 1993.

Carson, D.A., Douglas J. Moo and Leon Morris. *An Introduction to the New
Testament*. Rev. ed. Grand Rapids, MI: Zondervan, 1994.

Chadwick, Henry. *The Early Church*. New York: Pelican, 1964.

Clark, Elizabeth and Herbert Richardson. *Women and Religion: A Feminist
Sourcebook of Christian Thought*. New York: Harper and Row, 1977.

Copleston, Frederick. *A History of Christian Philosophy in the Middle Ages*.
London: Sheed and Ward, 1978.

Cross, Lawrence. *Eastern Christianity: The Byzantine Tradition*. Philadelphia:
E.J. Dwyer, 1988.

Dillenberger, John and Claude Welch. *Protestant Christianity. Interpreted
Through Its Development*. 2nd ed. New York: Macmillan, 1988.

Ferguson, Everett. *Encyclopedia of Early Christianity*. New York: Garland,
1990.

Hillerbrand Hans J., ed. *Christianity: The Illustrated History*. London: Duncan
Baird Publishers, 2008.

Jedin, Hubert. *The Church in the Modern World*. New York: Crossroad, 1993.

Johnson, Paul. *A History of Christianity*. New York: Atheneum, 1976.

Lossky, Vladimir. *The Mystical Theology of the Eastern Church*. London: James
Clarke, 1968.

Magill, Frank and Ian McGreal, eds. *Christian Spirituality: The Essential
Guide to the Most Influential Spritual Writings of the Christian Tradition*. San
Francisco: Harper and Row, 1988.

McGinn, Bernard. *The Foundations of Mysticism*. New York: Crossroad, 1992.

McGrath, Alister E. *Christian Theology: An Introduction*. Oxford: Blackwell,
1996.

McLaren, Robert Bruce. *Christian Ethics: Foundations and Practice*. Englewood
Cliffs, NJ: Prentice-Hall, 1994.

Porter, J.R. *The Illustrated Guide to the Bible*. London and New York: Duncan
Baird Publishers and Oxford University Press, 1995.

Porter, J.R. *Jesus Christ*. London and New York: Duncan Baird Publishers
and Oxford University Press, 1999.

Porter, J.R. *The Lost Bible*. London and New York: Duncan Baird Publishers
and Oxford University Press, 2001.

Porter, J.R. *The New Illustrated Companion to the Bible*. London: Duncan Baird
Publishers, 2003.

Quebedeaux, Richard. *The New Charismatics: The Origins, Development, and
Significance of Neo-Pentecostalism*. New York: Doubleday, 1976.

Raitt, Jill, ed. *Christian Spirituality*. 3 vols. New York: Crossroad, 1985–1989.

Self, David. *High Days and Holidays: Celebrating the Christian Year*. Oxford:
Lion, 1993.

Southern, R.W. *Western Society and the Church in the Middle Ages*. New York:
Penguin, 1970.

INDEX

Page numbers in **bold** refer to major references: page numbers in *italics* refer to captions.

112

ACKNOWLEDGMENTS AND PICTURE CREDITS

Unless cited otherwise here, text extracts are out of copyright or the product of the author's own translation.

The Scripture quotations contained herein are from the New Revised Standard Version Bible, copyright © 1989 by the Division of Christian Education of the National Council of the Churches of Christ in the U.S.A., and are used by permission. All rights reserved.

The following additional sources have kindly given their permission.

Aspects of the Divine, p.32: from *The Oecumenical Documents of the Faith* by T.H. Bradley and F.W. Green. Methuen: London, 1950, p.85ff.

Sacred Persons, p.52: from the angelus of Pope John Paul II, September 5, 1999, courtesy of the Catholic Information Network at www.cin.org/jp2/jp990905.html

Sacred Space, p.72: from *Eusebius: Church history, Life of Constantine the Great, and Oration in praise of Constantine* by Ernest Cushing Richardson (The Bagster translation, 1890) in *A Select Library of the Nicene and Post-Nicene Fathers of the Christian Church*, Volume 1, edited by P. Schaff and H. Wace. Reprinted by William B. Eerdmans: Grand Rapids, Michigan, 1986, p.162.

Death and the Afterlife, p.94: from *The First and Second Prayer Books of Edward VI* [*Book of Common Prayer*].

Introduced by Edgar C.S. Gibson. J.M. Dent and E.P. Dutton: London and New York, 1910.

Society and Religion, p.104: from *The Woman's Bible* by Elizabeth Cady Stanton (Foreword by Maureen Fitzgerald). Northeastern University Press: Boston, 1993, pp.14–15.

The publisher would like to thank the following people, museums, and photographic libraries for permission to reproduce their material. Every care has been taken to trace copyright holders. However, if we have omitted anyone we apologize, and will, if informed, make corrections in any future edition.
Page 2 Getty images/Stone/Joe Cornish; 8 Corbis SABA/Thomas Hartwell; 10 AKG images/Chilander monastery, Mount Athos; 16 AKG images/Aachen Cathedral; 22 Art Archive/National Gallery Budapest/ Dagli Orti (A); 26 Bridgeman Art Library/Alinari/Santa Maria della Vittoria, Rome; 34 AKG/Joseph Martin; Convent of St. Thomas, Avila; 38 AKG images/British Library; 44 Magnum Photos/ Susan Meiselas; 48 AKG images/ Erich Lessing/Uffizi; 54 AKG images/Gemäldegalerie, Berlin; 58 Corbis/Richard T. Nowitz; 62 Sonia Halliday Photographs; 67 Corbis/Bob Krist; 74 Corbis/Hanan Isachar; 78 Corbis/Ted Spiegel; 88 Corbis/Charles & Josette Lenars; 92 AKG images/Erich Lessing; 96 Corbis/ Bettmann; 100 Magnum Photos/Abbas